Hello, Family Members,

Learning to read is one of the most important accomplishments of early childhood. **Hello Reader!** books are designed to help children become skilled readers who like to read. Beginning readers learn to read by remembering frequently used words like "the," "is," and "and"; by using phonics skills to decode new words; and by interpreting picture and text clues. These books provide both the stories children enjoy and the structure they need to read fluently and independently. Here are suggestions for helping your child *before*, *during*, and *after* reading:

Before

- Look at the cover and pictures and have your child predict what the story is about.
- Read the story to your child.
- Encourage your child to chime in with familiar words and phrases.
- Echo read with your child by reading a line first and having your child read it after you do.

During

- Have your child think about a word he or she does not recognize right away. Provide hints such as "Let's see if we know the sounds" and "Have we read other words like this one?"
- Encourage your child to use phonics skills to sound out new words.
- Provide the word for your child when more assistance is needed so that he or she does not struggle and the experience of reading with you is a positive one.
- Encourage your child to have fun by reading with a lot of expression . . . like an actor!

After

- Have your child keep lists of interesting and favorite words.
- Encourage your child to read the books over and over again. Have him or her read to brothers, sisters, grandparents, and even teddy bears. Repeated readings develop confidence in young readers.
- Talk about the stories. Ask and answer questions. Share ideas about the funniest and most interesting characters and events in the stories.

I do hope that you and your child enjoy this book.

—Francie Alexander
Chief Education Officer,
Scholastic's Learning Ventures

For Abigail and Isabel: two young shining stars
—C.R. and P.R.

For David and Lynn
—C.S.

Special thanks to Paul Sieswerda of the
New York Aquarium for his expertise.

Go to scholastic.com for web site information
on Scholastic authors and illustrators.

ISBN: 0-439-33209-5

Text copyright © 2002 by Connie and Peter Roop.
Illustrations copyright © 2002 by Carol Schwartz.
All rights reserved. Published by Scholastic Inc.
SCHOLASTIC, HELLO READER!, CARTWHEEL BOOKS, and associated logos
are trademarks and/or registered trademarks of Scholastic Inc.

Library of Congress Cataloging-in-Publication Data
Roop, Connie.
    Starfish : stars of the sea / by Connie and Peter Roop ; illustrated by Carol Schwartz.
        p. cm. — (Hello reader! Science—Level 1)
    Summary: Simple rhyming text describes the characteristics and behavior of starfish.
    ISBN: 0-439-33209-5 (pbk.)
        1. Starfishes—Juvenile literature. [1. Starfishes.] I. Schwartz, Carol, 1954-ill. II.
    Title. III. Hello science reader! Level 2.
QL384.A8 R66 2002
593.9'3—dc21   2001040060

10 9 8 7 6 5 4 3 2   02 03 04 05 06

Printed in the U.S.A.   24
First printing, May 2002

Starfish
Stars
of the Sea

by Connie and Peter Roop
Illustrated by Carol Schwartz

Hello Reader! Science—Level 1

SCHOLASTIC INC.

New York   Toronto   London   Auckland   Sydney
Mexico City   New Delhi   Hong Kong   Buenos Aires

Under the sea,
along the shore,

live hundreds of starfish
on the ocean floor.

Starfish who live
on the ocean bed
are purple, orange,
brown, and red.

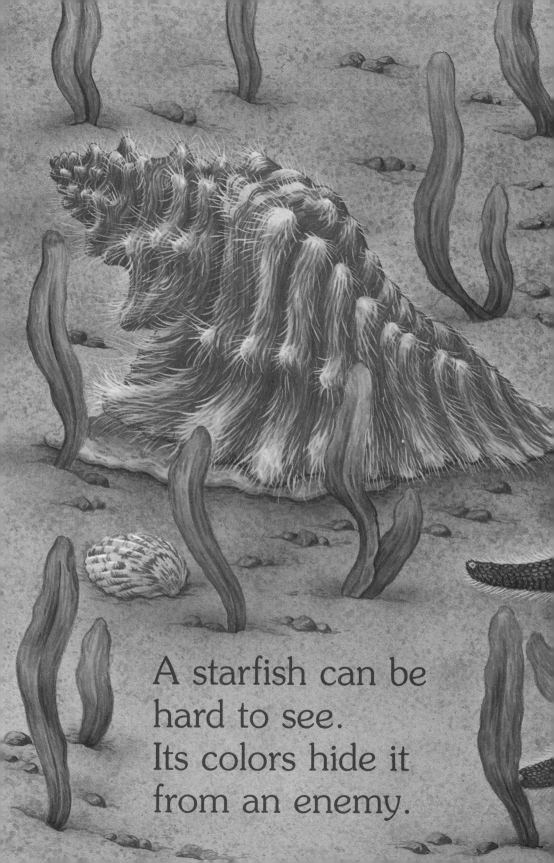

A starfish can be
hard to see.
Its colors hide it
from an enemy.

Starfish bodies have
no bones,
so starfish can crawl
into hidden homes.

Even if enemies do attack,
starfish are lucky . . .

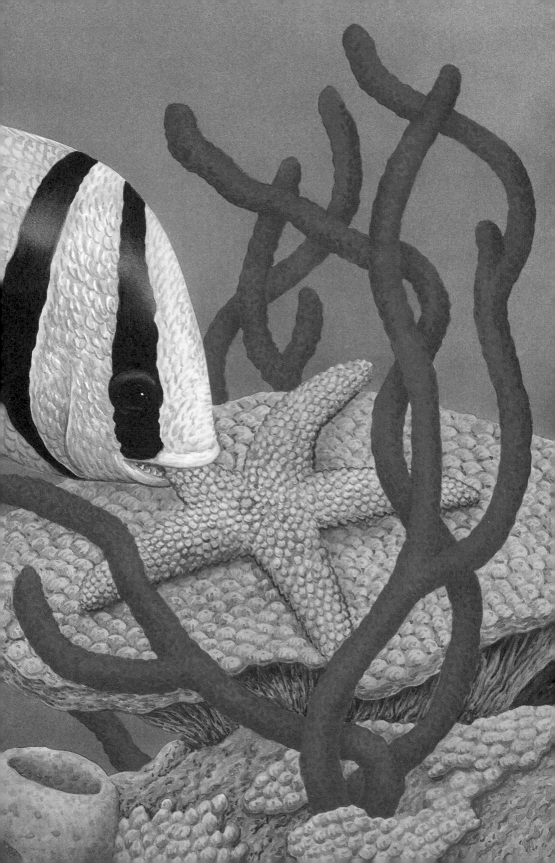

their arms grow back!

A starfish arm
is called a ray.
A spot on its tip
tells night from day.

Suckers help starfish
walk and crawl
and cling tightly to shells
or a rocky wall.

Rays are like fingers.
They touch and they feel . . .

as starfish hunt
for a shellfish meal.

A starfish holds
a shellfish tight,
then pulls it open
with all its might.

Starfish eat without
any teeth.
Their mouths are hidden
underneath.

Starfish are sometimes
called sea stars.
That's their other name.

But whether you call them
starfish or sea stars,
their lives are just the same.